THE REAL ESTATE AGENT SUCCESS SERIES, BOOK 1

REAL ESTATE AGENT STARTER GUIDE

FROM LICENSE TO LISTINGS

BY MALCOM LANE

Published by Lane Estates Publishing

www.LaneEstatesPublishing.com

ISBN: 978-1-968447-00-7

First Edition: June 2025

The information contained in this book is provided for educational and informational purposes only. The author and publisher assume no responsibility for errors, inaccuracies, or omissions. The content is not intended as legal, financial, or professional advice; readers should consult qualified professionals for such advice.

Cover design by Malcom Lane

DEDICATION

This book is dedicated to every dreamer who chose action.

To the new agents trying to figure it all out.
To the ones who feel overlooked, underestimated, or unsure.
To the grinders building their business one call, one showing, one deal at a time.

And most of all—to my family, especially my mother, Robin Lane, whose strength, sacrifice, and unconditional love gave me the courage to bet on myself. Every move I make is to honor you.

This is for us. This is legacy.

TABLE OF CONTENTS

PROLOGUE

A month after I hung my "Licensed Agent" plaque on the wall, my cousin Eunique Lane came to me—equal parts excited and terrified. She was a first-time buyer with a hundred questions and no roadmap. I didn't have one either. What I did have was a promise: I would learn fast and guide her every step of the way.

Our first offer landed on a house we both loved—but the inspection revealed serious issues the owner refused to fix. It stung, but we backed out the contract and pressed on. That setback forced me to dive deep into contracts, negotiation strategies, and down-payment assistance programs—all in record time. By deal two, I negotiated $5,000 in seller concessions and secured down-payment assistance that brought Eunique's closing costs down to just $100. The house appraised above our offer, gifting her instant equity— and after a few value-driving remodels, that equity swelled by another $10,000 in less than a year.

That whirlwind experience taught me three things: real estate is as much about perseverance as it is paperwork; every "no" is just the first step toward a better "yes"; and, most importantly, that the right agent can change someone's life. This guide is that roadmap I didn't have—built from real trials, wins, and lessons learned on the ground. Let's get started.

CHAPTER 1: GETTING LICENSED

THE REAL START

"Real estate is not just a career — it's a lifestyle. And your license is the entry ticket, not the finish line."
 — **Tiffanie Davis**, Real Estate Developer & Investor

Welcome to the Beginning

Passing your real estate exam is a major milestone. You studied, sacrificed, and focused — and now you've earned your license. But as real as that accomplishment feels, the truth is: this is just the beginning.

Your license is a tool, not a trophy. And if you don't know how to use it, it'll collect dust. The good news? You don't have to figure it all out alone. This chapter will walk you through the real start — how to think, act, and move like a real estate professional from day one.

The First 30 Days: Lay Your Foundation

Many new agents make the mistake of thinking things will fall into place automatically after getting licensed. But success in real estate is **intentional** — it takes strategy, consistency, and relentless self-promotion.

Here are the moves I recommend:

- **Choose your lane.** Are you more drawn to buyers, investors, luxury, commercial, or rentals? Start narrowing your niche early.

- **Pick the right brokerage.** Choose a team that aligns with your values and offers mentorship. Not every brokerage is built the same.

- **Study your market.** Know the average home prices, days on market, and hottest zip codes in your area.

- **Brand yourself.** Create your social media handles, take a professional photo, order business cards, and update your bio everywhere.

- **Talk to people.** Real estate is a contact sport. The more people who know what you do, the more likely you'll get business.

The Hustle Mindset

You're not just an agent — you're a business owner now. That means you have to:

- Set daily goals (calls made, people followed up with, properties studied)

- Track your numbers

- Invest in your growth

- Push past the fear of being "new"

Don't fall into comparison traps or wait until you "feel ready." Start messy. Learn as you go. Even your mistakes will teach you something valuable.

CHAPTER 1
REFLECTION & ACTION STEPS

1. What's your "why" for getting into real estate?

_____

_____

2. What niche are you most interested in and why?

_____

_____

3. Write a simple script you can say when someone asks what you do:

"Hey, I'm a licensed real estate professional helping people buy, sell, or invest in property right here in [City]. If you ever have a question or know someone who needs help — I'm your guy."

Write your version:

_____

_____

4. Make a list of 10 people to contact this week:

_____

_____

_____

CHAPTER 2: BUILDING YOUR BRAND

"You are the brand. People do business with people they know, like, and trust."
— *Egypt Sherrod, Real Estate Broker & Host of Married to Real Estate*

Who Are You in This Business?

You're not just a real estate agent — you're a brand. In this industry, people don't hire you because you have a license. They hire you because they believe in your energy, your knowledge, and your story.

Think of your brand as your reputation on display. It tells people:

- What you stand for

- Who you serve

- Why you're different

If you're forgettable, you're invisible. But if you build a strong, authentic brand — people will remember you, refer you, and respect you.

Find Your Voice

Your brand starts with **clarity**:

- Who is your ideal client?

- What neighborhoods or markets do you know best?

- Are you formal or laid back?

- Do you focus on first-time buyers, investors, or high-end listings?

Consistency across your Instagram, website, emails, and in-person interactions builds **trust**. If your social media is polished but you're disorganized in person — the brand breaks down.

Tools to Build Your Brand

Here are 5 brand-building moves to make this week:

1. **Create a professional email signature** with your name, title, phone number, and links.

2. **Record a short video intro** explaining who you are and how you help people.

3. **Design a social media content plan** — mix value, personality, and testimonials.

4. **Use a consistent color palette, font and tell your story** on all your materials, People connect with stories more than stats**.**

Branding Mistakes to Avoid

- Looking like everyone else

- Only posting listings with no educational content

- Using low-quality images or outdated headshots

- Neglecting your Google presence (create a business profile!)

CHAPTER 2
REFLECTION & ACTION STEPS

1. What do you want people to feel when they think of your name in real estate?

_____

2. Who is your ideal client? What's their lifestyle or challenge?

_____

3. Describe your brand in 3 words (ex: trustworthy, bold, resourceful):

_____

4. Write your brand intro sentence:
"I help [client type] in [location] [solve problem or achieve result] by [what makes you unique]."

Write your version:

_____

5. Make a list of your branding priorities this month:

- Get new photos

- Create a video intro

- Update bio

- Design Canva templates

- Launch website or linktree

CHAPTER 3: YOUR FIRST LISTINGS & CLIENTS

"Wealth is built brick by brick — one deal, one client, one relationship at a time."
    — Ashley Hamilton, Real Estate Entrepreneur

The Hustle Begins Here

This is the moment most new agents either **gain confidence** or **give up**.

You don't need a huge following. You don't need to be perfect.
You need to be **visible**, **available**, and **valuable** to someone. Start there.

Getting your first clients is about putting your name and purpose in the right places and **being brave enough to ask for the opportunity**.

Who Do You Already Know?

Your first few clients are likely already in your circle. Reach out to:

- Friends and family

- Church members

- Former coworkers

- Local business owners

- Sorority/fraternity brothers and sisters

Let them know you're licensed and ready to serve. But **don't just say you're a realtor** — say *how* you help and who you specialize in.

Example:
"Hey! I just launched my real estate business helping first-time buyers find their first homes in Broward County. If you or someone you know is thinking about buying or renting, send them my way!"

Strategies That Work

1. **Social Media Announcements**
   Post your new license status, behind-the-scenes videos, and share client success stories (even if they're from your team or office).

2. **Business Cards with Purpose**
   Hand out cards everywhere — but follow up. The magic is in the follow-up, not the handoff.

3. **Attend Networking Events**
   Pull up with confidence. Introduce yourself as the go-to agent in your area. People are always looking to buy, rent, or invest.

4. **Host a Free First-Time Buyer Workshop**
   Online or in-person. Partner with a mortgage lender. Make it educational and personal.

5. **Open Houses**
   Volunteer to host them, even if they're not your listing. You'll meet real buyers face-to-face.

Common Mistakes to Avoid

- Waiting for leads to come to you

- Not following up within 24–48 hours

- Being scared to talk about real estate publicly

- Forgetting to add value before asking for a sale

CHAPTER 3
REFLECTION & ACTION STEPS

1. Who are 10 people you can reach out to today?

   _____

2. What's your "I help" statement (write a fresh version if needed):

   _____

3. What platform will you use to stay consistent with content?
   - ☐ Instagram
   - ☐ Facebook
   - ☐ TikTok
   - ☐ LinkedIn
   - ☐ Email Newsletter

4. What's one event or opportunity you can attend or host this month?

   _____

5. What can you give to potential clients right now — knowledge, tools, inspiration?

   _____

CHAPTER 4: OPEN HOUSES & MARKETING YOUR LISTINGS

"Marketing is not a luxury in real estate — it's the difference between listings that sit and listings that sell."
— Quiana Watson, Broker & Real Estate Branding Expert

It's Not Just a House — It's a Story

When it comes to marketing, you're not selling walls and windows.
You're selling the **lifestyle**, the **neighborhood**, and the **dream**.

Whether it's your own listing or you're hosting an open house for another agent, your job is to make the property unforgettable.

Prepping for the Perfect Open House

1. **Know the Property Inside and Out**
   Study the upgrades, comps, schools, and community. Be ready for questions.

2. **Create a Vibe**
   Use music, air fresheners, and snacks to make the space inviting. You're not just selling a home — you're hosting a moment.

3. **Signage Matters**
   Place branded open house signs early and strategically — especially at major intersections. Include your phone number or QR code.

4. **Capture Emails at the Door**
   Use a sign-in sheet or iPad to collect contact info for follow-up.

5. **Go Live or Post Real-Time Updates**
   Stream short walk-throughs on Instagram or Facebook Live. Tag the location and invite your audience.

Creative Ways to Market a Listing

- **Professional Photos + Short Form Video Tours**
  Quality visuals are essential. Use vertical video for Reels and TikToks.

- **Highlight Local Amenities**
  Restaurants, schools, parks — sell the lifestyle.

- **Tell a Story in the Caption**
  Don't just say "3/2 in West Park."
  Try: "Imagine waking up in this light-filled 3-bedroom just 5 minutes from the beach... 🏝 "

- **Use Email & Text Campaigns**
  Send listing blasts to your personal contacts, other agents, and your buyer list.

- **Partner With Local Businesses**
  Put flyers in barbershops, beauty salons, or coffee shops. Offer free promo for cross-marketing.

Tips for Agents Without Listings Yet

- **Offer to Market Other Agents' Listings**
  Most will say yes if you're professional and respectful.

- **Document Your Journey**
  Post content as if you're already the go-to agent.
  Confidence builds credibility.

- **Create a "Dream Listing" Post**
  Feature a home you'd love to represent and ask your
  audience if they know anyone selling something
  similar.

CHAPTER 4
REFLECTION & ACTION STEPS

1. What type of listings do you want to specialize in?

_____

2. What's your Open House Prep Checklist?

☐ Clean

☐ Staged

☐ Music & Scent

☐ Signs Up

☐ Sign-In Sheet/iPad Ready

☐ Water & Snacks

3. What's your content plan when you get a listing?

_____

4. Name one creative way you'll market your next (or future) listing:

_____

5. Who can you collaborate with to expand your reach?

_____

CHAPTER 5: BUILDING RELATIONSHIPS & GETTING REFERRALS

"Your network is your net worth. Every conversation is a chance to plant a seed."
> — Eric Thomas, Motivational Speaker

Real Estate Is a Relationship Business

Long before you're closing deals consistently, you need people to trust you. That trust comes from showing up, staying consistent, and creating *real connections* — not just transactions.

Referrals will become your #1 source of business... if you build the right habits now.

The Relationship-Building Formula

1. **Be a Resource — Not a Salesperson**
   Share market updates, credit tips, and homeownership hacks — even if they're not ready to buy.

2. **Follow Up Intentionally**
   Check in on birthdays, congratulate job promotions, and send home anniversaries. These touches *matter*.

3. **Stay Visible**
   Be active on social, show your face in the community, and don't let people forget what you do.

4. **Ask for the Referral, the Right Way**
   Try this:
   "If you know anyone looking to buy, sell, or invest — I'd be honored to help. Just connect us!"

Turning Clients into Connectors

Treat every client like a VIP, whether it's a rental or a mill on-dollar deal. A great experience leads to word-of-mouth — and that's the most powerful marketing you can't buy.

Make it easy for them to refer you:

- Send a shareable contact card or Instagram post.

- Offer a "thank you" gift or referral incentive.

- Remind them with value, not pressure.

Plant Seeds in Unexpected Places

- **Your Barber or Loctician** – They talk to *everybody*.

- **Local Church or Community Leaders** – Ask to leave flyers or speak briefly.

- **Old Classmates & Teachers** – Reconnect and offer your expertise.

Keep showing up. Sometimes people are watching you for *months* before they reach out — or refer you to someone else.

CHAPTER 5
REFLECTION & ACTION PROMPTS

1. What's one relationship you need to re-nurture this week?

   _____

2. How will you stay top-of-mind with your sphere of influence?

   _____

3. Write out your go-to referral script or message:

   _____

4. Who are your top 5 connectors? How can you thank or support them?

   - _____

   - _____

   - _____

   - _____

   - _____

5. What small gift or gesture can you offer to referrals?

   _____

CHAPTER 6: TIME MANAGEMENT & STAYING CONSISTENT

"Consistency breeds trust. Show up every day, and your clients will show up for you."
— *Tiffany Aliche, "The Budgetnista"*

Why Time Management Matters in Real Estate

Real estate doesn't come with a clock-in and clock-out system — that's both a blessing and a challenge. You're your own boss, but that means success depends on your **systems**, **habits**, and how well you protect your time.

Without structure, it's easy to confuse "busy" with "productive." Top agents don't just work hard — they work smart.

Mastering the Real Estate Schedule

Here's a simple breakdown to start building your daily rhythm:

- **Morning (8am–11am):** Lead generation, follow-ups, market research

- **Midday (11am–2pm):** Client meetings, showings, emails

- **Afternoon (2pm–5pm):** Content creation, paperwork, training

- **Evening (5pm–7pm):** Social media engagement, recap tasks, prep for tomorrow

You don't have to follow this exactly — but you *do* need a flow.

Consistency > Intensity

You don't need to grind 24/7. What matters most is showing up consistently, *especially* when you don't feel like it.

Use time blocks. Set reminders. Treat your goals like appointments you can't miss.

Remember: Momentum builds *compound interest* in your business.

Set Realistic Weekly Goals

Here are a few examples of consistent, manageable goals:

- Contact 10 leads per day

- Post 3 times a week on Instagram

- Attend 1 networking event a week

- Review the MLS every morning

- Set 1 showing or buyer consultation per week

Use Systems to Stay Organized

Tools to consider:

- **CRM (Customer Relationship Manager):** Track leads & clients

- **Google Calendar or iCal:** Block time for key tasks

- **Trello or Notion:** Manage your pipeline & market ng plan

- **Notes app:** Brain dump and plan content ideas on the go

CHAPTER 6
REFLECTION & ACTION PROMPTS

1. What time of day are you most focused and productive?

   _____

2. What's one distraction you need to remove this week?

   _____

3. Which days and times will you dedicate to lead generation?

   _____

4. Write your ideal weekday schedule:

   • Morning: [_____]

   • Midday: [_____]

   • Afternoon: [_____]

   • Evening: [_____]

5. What task are you avoiding that you need to make a habit?

   _____

CHAPTER 7: STAYING MOTIVATED WHEN BUSINESS IS SLOW

"You may encounter many defeats, but you must not be defeated."
— Maya Angelou

The Reality of Slow Seasons

There will be seasons where the phone stops ringing. Deals fall through. Listings sit. Clients ghost you. It's normal — but it's also where most agents give up.

The agents who succeed long-term don't wait for motivation; they **create structure** and **stay visible** even when no one's watching.

What to Do When It's Quiet

Instead of stressing about what isn't happening, double down on what you *can* control:

- **Refine your systems** — Update your CRM, email templates, and follow-up scripts.

- **Create content** — Teach, document your process, and post consistently.

- **Learn your market** — Dive into MLS trends, property analysis, and niche areas.

- **Revisit leads** — Go back to your list and send a check-in or offer value.

Remember: **quiet seasons are building seasons.**

Visibility Beats Perfection

Even if you don't have a new deal to post, show up. Show your face. Talk about what you're learning. Showcase the behind-the-scenes.

People don't just follow success — they follow growth, hustle, and heart.

Check Your Mindset

Ask yourself:

- Am I comparing my journey to someone else's highlight reel?

- Am I measuring progress only by closed deals?

- Am I giving myself credit for the small wins?

This business is mental warfare. Feed your mind with positivity, community, and daily wins — even if they're small.

Rebuild with Intention

If it's slow, take the opportunity to:

- Rebrand your marketing

- Upgrade your photos or videos

- Build partnerships with lenders, inspectors, stagers, or contractors

- Reassess your niche or ideal client

Slow times force you to **level up** — use them to become the agent your future clients will trust.

CHAPTER 7
REFLECTION & ACTION PROMPTS

1. What's one thing I can improve during this slow season?

_____

2. How will I stay visible even when I don't have new deals?

_____

3. What past client or lead should I reconnect with today?

_____

4. What skill or knowledge should I double down on this month?

_____

5. Write one affirmation or mantra to repeat daily:

_____

CHAPTER 8: BUILDING A BRAND THAT ATTRACTS CLIENTS

"You are your best product — package it, protect it, and promote it."
— Issa Rae

More Than a Logo: What Your Brand Really Is

Your brand isn't just colors, fonts, or a logo. It's your energy, your story, your voice, and how you make people feel when they interact with you — online or in person.

For me, I realized early that my brand had to reflect not just my professionalism, but my roots. My upbringing in Carver Ranches, my passion for service, and my dream of turning real estate into legacy — that all became part of how I present myself.

When people work with you, they aren't just hiring an agent. They're aligning with a personality, a vibe, a mission.

The Foundation of a Strong Personal Brand

Here's what your brand should always communicate:

1. **Trust** – You show up. You follow through. You educate and empower.

2. **Relatability** – Your audience should feel like you "get them."

3. **Consistency** – Visually and verbally, your message and aesthetic should align.

4. **Expertise** – Through your content and conversations, show your knowledge without being overbearing.

5. **Authenticity** – People can spot fake energy from miles away. Be you, unapologetically.

How My Brand Began

I didn't have everything figured out when I started. But I did have my story.

When I helped my cousin Eunique Lane buy her first home — just a month after getting licensed — I learned fast. I didn't have all the answers, but I kept showing up and doing the research. That drive and heart became my brand before I ever picked brand colors or logos.

People started saying things like:

- "You really care."

- "You make it easy to understand."

- "You're always grinding."

Those became the building blocks of my brand. Not a Canva post — but **reputation**.

Content is Currency

In this digital era, your **Instagram, YouTube, TikTok, LinkedIn — that's your storefront**. If your last post was three months ago, and you're wondering why no leads are coming in, now you know.

You don't need to be an influencer. But you do need to **document the journey**:

- Walkthroughs

- Neighborhood tours

- Real estate tips

- Client wins and lessons

- Your story

People want to do business with real people — not flyers.

3 Questions to Build Your Brand Voice

1. What are 3 things I want to be known for?

2. What's one life experience that shaped my journey?

3. What do I offer that others don't?

Answer those, and you'll find your tone, message, and mission.

Stay Consistent, Stay Recognizable

Once you know who you are and what you stand for:

- Use a consistent color palette

- Get a professional headshot

- Choose a tone (fun, professional, inspiring?) and stick with it

- Keep your bio and link-in-bio updated

- Post with intention

CHAPTER 8
REFLECTION & ACTION PROMPTS

1. What does my brand say about me right now?

_____

2. Who is my ideal client and what do they value?

_____

3. How can I use my personal story to connect with my audience?

_____

4. What type of content do I enjoy creating?

_____

5. What's one brand update I'll make this week?

_____

CHAPTER 9: MASTERING THE ART OF FOLLOW-UP

"The fortune is in the follow-up."
— Jim Rohn

Why Follow-Up Matters More Than You Think

In real estate, your initial conversation is only the beginning. The deal rarely closes on the first call, DM, or showing. In fact, most clients need **7–10 touches** before they're ready to do business.

But too many agents give up after just one.

Follow-up isn't about being pushy — it's about being present, helpful, and consistent. It shows you care, that you're serious, and that you're **a professional who keeps their word**.

How I Learned the Power of Patience

Early in my career, I worked with a buyer who told me she "wasn't really ready yet." Instead of moving on, I added her to my CRM, set a reminder, and followed up every few weeks with market updates and helpful tips.

Eight months later, she called and said:
"You're the only one who kept in touch. I want to work with you."

That deal turned into a $10K commission — just because I didn't forget about her.

Your Follow-Up Blueprint

1. **First Contact:**

    ◦ Immediately send a personalized message or email thanking them.

    ◦ Add them to your CRM with notes.

2. **Within 48 Hours:**

    ◦ Share something valuable (listings, a video, or a tip that fits their need).

3. **Weekly Touches:**

    ◦ Send updates, content, or even a check-in message.

    ◦ Don't overdo it — be helpful, not spammy.

4. **Monthly Nurture:**

    ◦ Share newsletters, personal wins, or invite them to events.

    ◦ Make it feel organic and relationship-based.

Best Tools for Follow-Up

• **CRM Tools**: Follow Up Boss, LionDesk, or your phone contacts with reminders.

• **Email Marketing**: Mailchimp or Flodesk for drip campaigns.

• **Social Media**: Instagram DMs, comments, story replies — they all count.

- **Texting**: Use templates, but personalize them.

Build a Follow-Up System You Can Stick With

Whether it's:

- Mornings for prospecting

- Follow-Up Fridays

- Weekly CRM reviews

Make follow-up a *non-negotiable*. If you can't automate it, at least schedule it. Consistency beats perfection.

CHAPTER 9
REFLECTION & ACTION PROMPTS

1. Who have I forgotten to follow up with this month?

_____

2. What is my current follow-up process — and is it working?

_____

3. What tool will I start using to stay organized?

_____

4. What's one message I can send today to reconnect with someone?

_____

CHAPTER 10: SCALING YOUR BUSINESS WITH SYSTEMS AND STRATEGY

"You can't grow what you don't measure."
— Carla Harris, Real Estate Professional

From Hustling to Scaling

In the beginning, most of us are running from appointment to appointment, trying to do everything ourselves. That works at first — but it's not sustainable if your goal is to grow. If you want to make six figures or more, or build something that lasts, you need to think in terms of **systems**.

Scaling isn't about doing more — it's about doing less *better*, through strategy, automation, and delegation.

What Does Scaling Look Like in Real Estate?

- Creating repeatable processes for lead generation

- Automating follow-up and client communication

- Hiring a transaction coordinator or VA

- Building referral systems that run on autopilot

- Leveraging marketing templates and CRMs

- Delegating administrative tasks to focus on revenue-driving activity

My Journey: From Chaos to Clarity

There was a time when I was juggling showings, writing contracts at midnight, and forgetting who I promised to follow up with. I had leads falling through the cracks.

Once I built out templates for my emails, hired my mom as my transaction coordinator, and created a lead intake system — everything changed. I closed more deals with less stress and finally had time to *grow* instead of just keep up.

Must-Have Systems to Scale

1. **CRM & Pipeline Tracking**

    - Track where every lead is in your process.

    - Examples: Follow Up Boss, Trello, Notion, or even a spreadsheet.

2. **Marketing & Content Calendar**

    - Plan out weekly posts, emails, videos, and stories ahead of time.

3. **Email & Text Templates**

    - Draft once. Use forever. Save hours each week.

4. **Outsourcing Admin Tasks**

    - Use a transaction coordinator (or train one in-house).

    - Delegate social media scheduling, data entry, or cold outreach.

5. **Automated Follow-Up**

- Use drip campaigns to nurture long-term leads.

6. **Finance & Budgeting System**

    - Know your numbers. Use QuickBooks, Excel, or an accountant.

The Mindset Shift: CEO vs Agent

Think like a CEO, not just an agent.
Ask yourself:

- What can be delegated?

- What can be automated?

- What absolutely requires *me*?

CHAPTER 10
REFLECTION & ACTION PROMPTS

1. What's one area of my business I can systemize this week?

_____

2. What's stopping me from delegating more?

_____

3. What's my current process for onboarding a new client? Can it be improved?

_____

4. Who can I hire or bring on to support my growth?

_____

CHAPTER 11: BUILDING YOUR BRAND IN THE DIGITAL AGE

"Your brand is what people say about you when you're not in the room."
     — Jeff Bezos

What Is a Brand and Why Does It Matter?

Your brand isn't just your logo or colors — it's the feeling people associate with your name. In real estate, where relationships and trust are everything, your personal brand is often the reason someone chooses you over another agent.

Whether you're in the room or not, your **online presence speaks for you.** That's why in today's digital-first world, building a strong brand is not optional — it's essential.

Personal Story: From Posts to Profits

When I first started, I posted because I felt like I had to. "Just sold," "new listing," "open house." It was robotic — and people scrolled past.

Everything changed when I started showing *me* — the behind-the-scenes, the journey, the wins and the struggles. I began getting DMs from people saying, "I feel like I know you," and that's when referrals started pouring in. My brand stopped being "a realtor" and started being *me* — someone they could trust.

Your Brand Pillars: What You Should Be Known For

To build a memorable brand, define 3–4 brand pillars. These are topics you consistently talk about or themes you're known for.

Examples:

- Real estate education

- Local community highlights

- Your journey & story

- Client success stories

- Financial empowerment

- Style or lifestyle tips

Content That Connects

You don't have to go viral. You just need to be *consistent* and *intentional.*

Post content that:

- Educates (buyer tips, seller checklists, market updates)

- Inspires (testimonials, quotes, your story)

- Connects (day-in-the-life, behind the scenes)

- Converts (call-to-action posts, limited-time offers, home tours)

Use video as much as possible. Reels, stories, and short-form content are king on Instagram, TikTok, and YouTube Shorts.

Digital Tools to Elevate Your Brand

- **Canva Pro**: For polished graphics & branded content

- **Later / Planoly**: Content scheduling

- **CapCut / InShot**: Easy video editing on mobile

- **Linktree / Stan Store**: One-click access to all your links

- **Brand Kit**: Keep consistent fonts, colors, and templates

CHAPTER 11
REFLECTION & ACTION PROMPTS

1. What are my top 3 brand pillars?

_____

2. What do I want people to *feel* when they come across my content?

_____

3. What's one piece of content I can create this week that tells my story?

_____

4. Do I have a consistent bio, profile pic, and call to action across platforms?

_____

CHAPTER 12: INVESTING IN REAL ESTATE & BUILDING GENERATIONAL WEALTH

"You can't pass down a 9 to 5, but you can pass down a deed."
— Garnika Lane-Pierre

Why Investing Should Be Part of Your Game Plan

Becoming a licensed agent opens the door to real estate, but investing unlocks the gate to *freedom*. Too many agents focus solely on transactions — working for commissions instead of building portfolios. The real money? It comes when you own.

Real estate investing isn't just for the wealthy. It's one of the most accessible tools to build wealth that you can *leverage, duplicate, and pass on*.

My First Investment: Learning by Doing

I'll never forget the first property I bought. It wasn't flashy, and I was nervous. I ran the numbers 20 times. But once I closed, I realized something: *I had just bought an income stream.* That one deal shifted my mindset forever. A few years later, after some renovations and tenant turnover, it appraised for over $40,000 more than I paid. That's equity. That's power.

Types of Real Estate Investments to Explore

- **Single-Family Rentals (SFRs)** – Easier to finance and manage, great for beginners.

- **Multi-Family Units** – Duplexes, triplexes, and quads allow you to house hack or multiply income.

- **Fix and Flips** – Higher risk, but big short-term gains if done right.

- **Short-Term Rentals (Airbnb/VRBO)** – Great in tourist areas, but needs solid systems.

- **Vacant Land** – Low entry cost, ideal for development or long-term hold.

Running the Numbers (Not the Emotions)

Before buying, analyze:

- Monthly cash flow (rent minus expenses)

- Estimated repairs and upgrades

- Long-term appreciation potential

- Property management costs

- ROI and cap rate

Don't just fall in love with the home — fall in love with the *deal*.

Leveraging Your License

As a realtor, you're already ahead:

- First access to deals

- Ability to run your own comps

- Networking with contractors and investors

- Cutting out commissions (or earning your own!)

If you're helping others buy homes, why not help yourself first?

Generational Wealth Starts with One Property

Many of us didn't grow up learning about equity, refinancing, or passive income. But once you learn it, you have a responsibility to *teach it* — and to create options for your family.

You don't need to buy 10 properties tomorrow. Just start with one. Let your first rental teach you. Let your second bring stability. By your third, you'll have a system.

CHAPTER 12
REFLECTION & ACTION PROMPTS

1. What's holding me back from buying my first or next property?

_____

2. Do I know my local rental market — and who's buying right now?

_____

3. What kind of investment strategy fits my current lifestyle best?

_____

4. Who in my network can mentor me, partner with me, or help fund a deal?

_____

CHAPTER 13: LEAVING A LEGACY – TURNING SUCCESS INTO SIGNIFICANCE

"The goal isn't more money. The goal is living life on your terms and helping others do the same."
— Malcom Lane

When I first got into real estate, it was about freedom. Freedom of time, freedom of money, and freedom to create the life I always envisioned. But somewhere along the journey, I realized something deeper—it's not just about what I build for myself. It's about what I leave behind for those who come after me.

Legacy is bigger than wealth. It's about impact. It's about how many people you help along the way. It's about changing the narrative in your family, in your community, and in your culture. And as a real estate professional, you're in one of the few industries where you can literally change lives—by helping people buy their first home, build generational wealth, or even launch their own careers.

From Hustle to Impact

Once your systems are tight, your pipeline is full, and the business is scaling—ask yourself: *"Now what?"* That's when the focus shifts from hustle to purpose.

Here are a few ways I've started thinking about legacy in my business:

- **Mentorship**: Whether it's a young agent or a family member, share what you know. You don't need to have all the answers. Just be real, be accessible, and be honest about the journey.

- **Ownership**: Encourage ownership in our communities —homes, land, businesses. Teach people that owning is power.

- **Representation**: Sometimes your greatest impact is simply being visible. Letting someone see that success is possible, that they belong in this room, too.

What Are You Building Beyond the Commission?

Your name holds weight. Your work is a reflection of your values. Every deal you close, every client you serve, every connection you build—it all adds up.

So don't just chase success. Chase significance.

Keep growing. Keep leveling up. But never forget to reach back.

Your Legacy Prompt:

Take a moment to reflect and write:

1. *What kind of legacy do I want to leave through my real estate career?*

2. *Who can I impact right now with the knowledge and experience I've gained?*

3. *What will my name represent 10, 20, or 50 years from now?*

FINAL WORD: KEEP PUSHING THE VISION

By Malcom Lane

If you've made it this far, thank you. That means something. You didn't just pick up this book—you showed up for your future. And that's what being a real estate professional is really about: showing up. Every day. Even when it's hard. Especially when it's hard.

I didn't write this book because I had all the answers—I wrote it because I know what it's like to start from the ground up. I know what it feels like to doubt yourself, to wait for the phone to ring, to wonder if this career was the right move. But I also know what it feels like to close that first deal, help someone buy their first home, and look in the mirror knowing you didn't give up.

The truth is, real estate is bigger than just buying and selling property—it's about building a legacy. For yourself. For your family. For your community. So no matter what chapter you're in right now—whether you're just getting started or looking to level up—I want you to keep pushing the vision.

Keep learning. Keep serving. Keep showing up. The world needs more leaders who lead with heart, hustle, and purpose. And I believe you're one of them.

I'll see you at the closing table.

— Malcom A. Lane

Author, Realtor, Investor, Dream Builder

ABOUT THE AUTHOR

Malcom Lane is a Florida-born entrepreneur, licensed real estate agent, and the founder of Lane Estates Management and Secure Lanes. Raised in Carver Ranches and a proud graduate of FAMU, Malcom's journey into real estate began with one mission: to build generational wealth and help others do the same.

He specializes in working with first-time buyers, investors, and sellers throughout South Florida and Georgia—empowering clients with knowledge, strategy, and real results. Malcom also coaches new agents, sharing the tools and mindset that helped him build his brand and close deals.

Beyond real estate, he's a tech founder developing apps for real estate, government contracting, and business efficiency at Secure Lanes. His passion for innovation, community, and legacy fuels everything he does.

Whether you're a new agent or someone looking to level up in life, Malcom's story and this guide are proof that with focus and execution, you can build the life you want—starting right where you are.

Connect with Malcom:
- Instagram: @LaneEstates
- Website: LaneEstatesPublishing.com
- Email: malcomlane@LaneEstatesPublishing.com

www.ingramcontent.com/pod-product-compliance
Lightning Source LLC
Chambersburg PA
CBHW071037050426
42335CB00051B/2382